Sell Your Home In a Tough Market - NOW!!!

Practical advice that gets results!

Crissie Cudd

iUniverse, Inc.
New York   Bloomington

Sell Your Home In a Tough Market - NOW!!!

Practical advice that gets results!

iUniverse books may be ordered through booksellers or by contacting:

iUniverse
1663 Liberty Drive
Bloomington, IN 47403
www.iuniverse.com
1-800-Authors (1-800-288-4677)

Because of the dynamic nature of the Internet, any Web addresses or links contained in this book may have changed since publication and may no longer be valid. The views expressed in this work are solely those of the author and do not necessarily reflect the views of the publisher, and the publisher hereby disclaims any responsibility for them.

ISBN: 978-1-4401-0459-6 (pbk)
ISBN: 978-1-4401-0460-2 (ebk)

Library of Congress Control Number: 2008941181

Printed in the United States of America

iUniverse rev. date: 11/05/08

Introduction

Why are you selling?

If this is a down market, why sell? Do you HAVE to sell? Does a job change require a move?

There are a lot of legitimate reasons to sell, even in a down market. Job changes, financial status, or family circumstances can all dictate a move. Just deciding you want a change may not be a good reason if it has serious financial consequences.

When selling a home it's important to determine what it is you hope to accomplish with the sale. Is the most important thing to make a lot of money, or to be able to move on to the next part of your life? Those are two very different motivations and it's essential to understand the differences.

If making a lot of money is your objective, then selling in a down market may not be an option. You may want to find a way to delay selling till the market improves. If moving on with your life is important, then the sale is all-important and price is secondary.

Identifying your prime motivation for selling will help when the times comes that you get a contract. Knowing what you are trying to accomplish will help when you have to decide how far you will bend on price or what terms you are willing to accept or even what timetable the contract will specify.

Just because this is a down market does not mean you must accept just any contract that comes your way. The price and terms must fit in with your goals and objectives. If you have done all the right things up to that point you'll be able to make a good decision when you have a contract to negotiate.

Market Definition

The term "market" describes the atmosphere that exists when buying or selling a home. The laws of supply and demand follow the market.

A "sellers" market is typically described as a "hot" market. There are relatively few homes for sale and they don't stay on the market for long. This low supply usually means that prices will rise.

A "buyers" market is a "down" market because there are more homes for sale than there are buyers and homes take longer to sell. Prices tend to drop as sellers compete for the few buyers available.

Selling your home in a down market is different than a "normal" market or a "hot" market. In a "hot" market, buyers are everywhere, there is a small supply of homes, and they sell in a matter of days or a few weeks. Supply and demand work in the seller's favor because every home gets shown and most sell quickly, regardless of condition or even price.

In a "normal" market there is still only a moderate supply of homes and a buyer may look at all the homes in an area and consider most of them.

In a "down" market there is simply too great a supply of homes for a buyer to see them all. Potential buyers will narrow down the search by price and eliminate based on the condition of the home, or the PERCEIVED condition of the home (more on that later).

Selling a home in a down market requires a different approach than in a hot or normal market. With so many homes on the market the seller has three challenges: to make sure the buyer has a favorable impression of the home, to make sure it is priced competitively, and to make sure the home gets seen.

You can sell your home with a real estate broker or sell it yourself. There will be details on those choices later in the book when we talk about exposure to the market. But whether or not you list with a broker or sell it yourself you still have to prepare the home for the market and price it correctly.

As a seller, you can't control the market. You can't control what the media is saying or what banks are charging. You can't change the location of your home, or the actual age of it.

So let's begin with what you *can* control.

Challenge #1 – A Favorable Impression

First Impressions Count

It may seem backwards to work on the appearance of the home first. However, you want to make sure that when the home is found that is shows at its best. *"You never get a second chance to make a first impression."*

You have to make your home look better than any other one for sale in the neighborhood – more appealing. Some of these suggestions are going to cost you money, but not as much as you think. Many of the suggestions will only cost you your time and most all of them will SAVE you money in the long run. These suggestions can reduce the length of time you need to market the home and some will even make the home sell for a greater price.

Why do many people choose a brand new home over a used one? The answer is "appeal". That new home looks fresh, clean, in good repair, and it has been arranged, or staged, in such a way as to maximize the good features and minimize the bad ones. For your home to compete in a "down" market it has to look as close to "model" perfect as it can get.

Many people make the mistake of selling a home "as is", with no repairs or cosmetic touch-ups. However, buyers typically look at what a home needs to have done and they mentally begin to subtract the cost for those changes from the listed price. Even if the seller has tried to price it with those things in mind, the buyer still makes deductions.

And here is the worst part of that. The buyer subtracts a much larger amount than is really necessary. Take carpet for example. You might be able to replace stained and worn carpet with a new, builder grade carpet for $3000. The buyer sees the old carpet and thinks, "This place needs new carpet. And if I'm going to replace it I'll want a nice grade of carpet with a nice pad. That's about

$6000." So if they make an offer on the home, they will knock $6,000 off their offer price for the carpet alone.

Paying for some improvements up front can actually result in a greater profit in the end for the seller.

Get a legal pad and pen and begin to walk through your home from curbside all the way through to the back yard and make notes. Here are the things to look for.

Outside the Home

Spend time on the outside of the home. Many people drive by a home before they decide if they want to see the inside. If the outside is a turn-off the customer will go no further. People assume that the *inside* of the home will be maintained the same way as the *outside* of the home. This goes back to the concept of the PERCEIVED condition of the home. People draw conclusions from first impressions.

Yard:

Start with the yard. Does the grass need fertilizing? Do you need a weed killer? Do you need to plant new grass or replace sod? You have time and these things don't get results overnight so start now.

If it's the time of year for leaves to fall, rake them up regularly. Unraked leaves make a home look neglected and can kill the grass underneath.

Trim bushes and trees so that no windows are blocked. You want to let in as much light as possible and you don't want to hide the features of the home. If there are diseased trees or bushes, or dead plants, have them removed.

Color helps, so where can you add flowers or plants with color? No matter what time of year or what part of the country there is always something blooming or that has colorful foliage that will enhance the appearance of the home.

Adding bedding plants that have color to the base of trees can make a drab yard more colorful and eye-catching.

If the mailbox is by the road, that's a good place to start adding details. A few inexpensive small plants that add color make a nice focal point. Of course, the mailbox and post should also look appealing. Replace a rusty or dented mailbox and repaint the post.

Then under the front windows and by the front door you may need to add plants to fill in bare spots or to soften the hard edges of the home.

It may go without saying, but since some people do it, it needs to be said: don't put fake flowers in your yard anywhere. They will hurt the appearance of the home instead of helping it.

In all the flower beds or around bushes, add mulch. It adds a richness and color to the yard. If the home is on the market for an extended period of time be sure to replace any mulch that washes away as needed.

On the other hand, don't go crazy. The yard that looks as though it will take a Master Gardener's license to maintain it will turn off some people. Keep it simple but make your home stand out among the other homes on the street in a nice way.

Throughout the time the home is on the market make sure the yard is mowed and edged, the plants trimmed and watered, leaves raked, and plants replaced as necessary on a regular basis.

Don't neglect the backyard either. If necessary, fill in bare spots with new sod. Add trees to a plain back yard. Put color or attractive bushes in the back yard as well.

Children's play sets that are being sold with the home need to be in good repair. Things that are not included should be removed so that the yard appears larger. If removing a swing set or trampoline leaves a bare spot in the lawn it must be filled and blended in with the rest of the yard.

If there is a fence, make sure it's in good repair and attractive. Paint or stain it, fix any parts that need it, and oil the gate hinges. People spend more time in the back yard than the front yard so you should make sure it shows well and looks appealing.

If you own a condo or townhome and have limited or no yard you can still make the roadside appearance more appealing with the use of potted plants. Without crowding the entryway, add a potted plant or group of plants for color and to soften the lines of the home and make it more inviting.

Pool area:

Pools must be maintained year round. Covers should be clean and equipment kept in good condition. Debris should be removed on a daily basis – you never know when someone will want to see the home.

Maintain the chemical balance in the water so that it looks fresh and appealing, no matter what the temperature or time of year. If the pool is drained keep it empty of debris and standing water.

The pool deck should have cracks repaired and the surface kept clean. There are paints made especially for pool decks and if yours is faded or stained that might be a good idea. Keep the color neutral.

Porches and decks:

No matter what the size, this is an important feature to the home. Outside furniture and accessories should always be clean and well-maintained. Get rid of worn out chairs and tables. Make sure the area isn't cluttered. Toys and hobbies need to be packed up and out of sight.

Potted plants add color and make the area look more livable. Make sure they are healthy and arranged tastefully and have no dirty spots around them. They should not overwhelm the area or block a great view.

The exterior of the home:

Paint is the obvious choice that makes a huge difference in the appearance of a home. Fresh paint in a color appropriate for the neighborhood and current trends is never a bad idea. However, it can't be done half way. Repainting must include trim, gutters, shutters, doors, and windows.

Is it necessary? Well, is the color faded? Is the paint stained or chipped? Then repainting is probably the answer. If painting is too costly or the need is borderline, there is an alternative – pressure washing. You can buy or rent a good electric pressure washer from your local home improvement store, plug it in, hook up the hose, and you're in business. There are companies you can hire for this if you lack the time or energy.

Pressure washing will take mildew off gutters and trim, remove many stains from walls, get rid of cobwebs, dirt, etc. It will also take off chipped and flaking paint so this isn't the answer if your home really does need repainting. And while we're on the topic of pressure washing, driveways, sidewalks, pool decks, wooden fences, and porches should also be pressure washed. Concrete will look brighter and newer and cracks will appear less obvious.

If the roof is stained and dirty pressure washing can make it look brand new (or at least better) but roofs should really be done by a professional.

Cracked window panes need to be replaced, as well as torn or missing screens. No windows should be painted shut and all should open with ease and without sound effects. A little WD-40 solves a lot of problems.

Front Entry:

The front entry to the home is a focal point that can't be ignored. A freshly painted front door that doesn't squeak is essential. The handle or knob should be shiny and bright and the lock should open smoothly. Depending on the look of the home, a door knocker or kick plate can enhance the look as well. New hardware isn't expensive and can make a positive first impression. Lastly, don't overlook the doormat. It should be fresh, not worn out, clean and inviting.

Garage:

Before we go inside the home let's tackle what is typically the most neglected part of the home – the garage. Customers will form an impression of the home by what they see in the garage.

First of all, clean it out. There needs to be adequate room for the appropriate amount of cars intended for its use. If there is still room for one or two bicycles and a moderate amount of tools then you're okay. Anything else goes into a rented storage unit, the garage of a close friend, or trash.

Make sure the garage door opens without squeaks, there is no rust or wood rot anywhere, and the floor isn't covered with stains. There are products at your local home improvement store to remove concrete stains and others to use to repaint it (be sure to use the right products or you'll create new problems.)

While we're at it, don't neglect repainting the walls in the garage if you do other painting. It can make the garage look larger and in better shape.

If the hot water heater, or the washer and dryer are in the garage make sure there is adequate room for them and that they are in good working order.

Storage units and wall hooks for tools or bicycles will make the area look more spacious and organized.

Inside the home

People will spend time or leave quickly depending on what they see when they walk in the door. Roomy, spacious homes have more appeal but even small homes can give that impression. Clean, well-lit, tidy homes are more appealing than cluttered, dark, or unkempt ones.

Making changes inside the home won't always result in a higher priced sale but it will make the difference in whether or not you even get an offer.

Before you replace anything in the home or make major improvements, check to see what other homes on the market in the area look like. This applies to floor coverings, appliances, cabinets, lighting, etc. It is possible to over-improve a home, meaning that the home has more improvements than a typical home in the area.

Being over-built for the area may make your home sell faster, but not necessarily for more money.

For example, if all the other homes in your neighborhood have laminate kitchen counters and you install granite, you will look more appealing to a potential buyer but they will probably not be willing to pay more than they would for one of the other homes.

Surveys across the country show that many home improvements result in less than half the money spent being recovered when it sells. However, the right home improvements can make the difference in whether or not it sells at all.

De-clutter:

Long before a customer notices improvements in the home, they notice size – or the perception of size. A small, uncluttered home will appear larger than a moderately sized home that is filled to the rafters with excess furniture, knick knacks, and personal belongings.

So here is the toughest advice in the book – *get rid of stuff.*

There are air conditioned storage units that can be rented for an affordable price in every area of the country. Instead of burdening family or friends with your excess, rent a unit and then put into it whatever items you need to remove from the home.

Valuables:

Never keep firearms, fine jewelry, or any cash in a home for sale. The risks are too great. Store them in a safe deposit box in a bank.

Prescription drugs can be a target of thieves that prey on sellers because drugs are so easily concealed and are easily marketable. Drugs should never be left in a medicine cabinet or bathroom drawer. They should be hidden in an obscure place in the home.

Collections:

Are there any collectors in the home? Pack up those valuable collections and get them out of sight. You don't want to risk losing a part of them to a light-fingered "guest". (Theft is not common in homes for sale, but because it does happen occasionally, you want to prevent it if possible.)

It doesn't matter if it's a collection of porcelain statues, dolls, or matchbooks, it's time to pack it away. Collections of any kind take up valuable room and they distract the customer from focusing on the home.

Video, DVD, and CD collections should be neat and orderly and should never dominate the room. The same applies to books. Shelves should never be completely full. Use bookends, a small plant, or just open space, to create breaks. This is a good time for another charity donation. If you can't part with any of them, then box them up and store them until you move to your new home.

Closets:

Next, tackle closets. Most people have clothes they never wear, so this is a good time to get rid of them. If they are worth donating to charity you'll pick up a tax deduction as well.

If clothing is out of season, box it up and get it out of the way. Put the out of season clothes into storage or at a friend's home. Line up your closet shoes on a shoe rack, on a shelf, or neatly on the floor. Get rid of those stacks of shoe boxes – they take up too much space.

Closets should look sparse – it makes them appear larger. People look for large closets. Demonstrating that you can cram a lot in has the opposite effect.

If you can't survive with the amount of clothes that leaves you, put some into suitcases under the bed and work with that. Or fold more and put them into dresser drawers. This is a short-term situation while your home is being sold and you can live with the inconvenience if it gets the job done.

Do this with every closet in every room. There can be no exceptions. You want the customer to remark, "This home has a lot of closet space!"

Kitchen:

This same task needs to take place in the kitchen as well. Pack up or throw out the mismatched glasses and all the plastic soft drink cups from fast food restaurants. Every single cabinet door should open to neatly arranged, small quantities of kitchen items. Every member of the household has to cooperate to keep it that way until the home is sold.

Small appliances should be limited to no more than one per counter. Put the rest under the cabinet, out of sight, or pack them away. Counters should be cleaned off and nearly bare. Towels and pot holders should be freshly cleaned, and if possible, new. Stained or faded accessories make a kitchen look old.

You're thinking that so far this is a pain in the neck and not worth it. Am I right? Sorry.

Customers reject homes that are cluttered or they offer less than they would otherwise.

Accessories:

Now you need to walk through each room. One wall hanging per wall or small group of pictures is plenty. If you have more than that, begin taking some down. Your art work and photographs should *accent* walls, not cover them up.

Now look at all the knick knacks sitting on surfaces throughout the home. Pack up most of them. Two or three per room in most cases is sufficient. You must be relentless in every area in the home. The smaller the room, the fewer the knick knacks.

Family photos should be kept to a bare minimum. It's harder for customers to envision themselves in the home when they see other people's faces staring back at them everywhere they look.

Children's Rooms:

Children's rooms can be a special challenge. You may need to buy colorful laundry baskets that can be used for quick clean-ups prior to a last minute showing of the home. Under the bed storage containers can be a good buy as well.

Involve the children in selling the home and make it a game. Prior to each showing, have the kids help tidy up. Then during the showing, go some place fun. Go to the park, the movies, out to eat or to shop. You'll get a lot more cooperation that way.

Staging:

Do the rooms still feel crowded? Is there too much furniture crammed in? This is difficult but you may have to remove some large pieces or excess items. Large furniture that dominates a room will make the room appear smaller.

Rooms should look as though they have one purpose, not several. So desks should not be in eat-in kitchens, and neither should TVs. Beds should only be in bedrooms. Game tables and equipment don't belong in living rooms. Eating areas should have eating furniture. Using rooms for things other than what was intended will give the customer the impression that the floor plan isn't workable.

Dining rooms and breakfast areas should look roomy so it might be a good idea to take out the extra leaf in the table and remove extra chairs.

A professional stager can rearrange your furniture and accessories to maximum advantage and come up with ideas that most people would never think of. This may be an expense that is worthwhile.

If you are considering hiring a professional stager, see examples of their work. Talk to their references. Ask about their training or certification credentials. Compare prices.

Many Realtors have also had professional staging training and some may be willing to stage your home for free or a reduced fee in exchange for listing the home with them. Evaluate all your choices before making a decision.

Lighting:

Every room should have as much natural light as possible. Go back outside and make sure no large bushes are blocking the light and trim them back or replace them with smaller ones.

Make sure all light bulbs are clean and dust-free and that you have enough light in each room for the home to show well on cloudy or rainy days. Consider switching to higher wattage bulbs if necessary.

A note on light fixtures: If there is a light fixture or ceiling fan in the home you don't plan to sell with the home, now is the time to take it down and replace it with something inexpensive. Never leave something for a customer to fall in love with that they can't have. It will come back to haunt you when the contract is contingent on that special piece being included.

If your window coverings block the light you may need to consider making changes there. You should pull back drapes (including sheers), open shutters, and raise blinds to let in natural light. Replace dark or heavy window coverings if necessary.

Floors:

No matter what kind of floor covering you have, it must be clean. Dirt, stains, scratches, etc. prevent your home from showing at its best. Each type of floor covering has its own pros and cons.

Never replace if you can clean or repair. The sales price of a home with "nice" floors and the same home with "great" floors may not be enough to warrant the expense of replacement.

Wood floors should look bright and shiny. Look long and hard because they may need refinishing. Professionals can be expensive and do-it-yourself refinishing can go bad in the wrong hands so make the right decision. If refinishing isn't needed or possible, then clean them thoroughly and polish them with a rented floor polisher.

Tile floors usually clean up well except for grout. Dirty or stained grout can make the entire floor look old and out of date. There are professionals who are able to steam clean the grout and may be able to make old stained grout look brand new. If you are considering this, let the professional do a demo on a small area that won't be too noticeable in case you decide not to go forward with the cleaning. One clean spot will only make the rest look worse.

Linoleum and vinyl are relatively easy to replace if there are tears or stains, but again, know what you are doing or get a pro.

Carpet that has ripples and bumps needs to be restretched by a carpet specialist. All carpet should be professionally cleaned before you put the home on the market. This is especially necessary if you have ever had pets or smokers living in the home. Many buyers have allergies that will pick up on the slightest carpet odors.

If the carpet is beyond cleaning or worn to a serious degree then replacement is necessary. Look for an inexpensive builder grade with a good pad in a lighter neutral color. Keep the quality appropriate to other homes for sale in the area. Overdoing it will not necessarily earn back its cost. However, going too cheap may make the home look inferior to the market and the buyer will still think the home needs new carpet.

Paint:

A freshly painted room in a light neutral color is always a good suggestion. Fresh paint makes the home look cleaner and smell new. Dark rooms look smaller. Strong colors make it harder for potential customers to envision their own possessions in them and look like more work and expense to move in.

It is better to have one neutral color throughout the home than a different color in every room. Accent walls may look great in a magazine or model home but they chop up a room in real life and turn off potential buyers.

You may think neutral paint colors are "boring" but your customer will see "new". It's one less thing they have to pay for or do immediately so it's one less deduction in their minds on the price.

If you can't paint or it isn't necessary, then do touch ups wherever they are needed. Repair and paint where wall hangings have come down. Clean smudges and scuff marks off walls.

Light switches and wall outlets should be clean as well, with no chips or cracks. Replace any that are less than perfect.

Clean:

Clean everything in the home as though your pickiest relative is coming for a visit. Not only should you do this before putting the home on the market, but it needs to be a continuing plan of action throughout the entire time the home is for sale.

Dirt, dust, fingerprints, mildew, stains, etc. represent dollar signs. If your customer sees any of them they begin to mentally deduct dollars. Human nature is such that people will not pay full price for what appears to be "used". Making your home appear brand new (even when it isn't) will get you a higher sales price.

Pets:

Pet smells need to be eliminated entirely. If necessary, switch to dry food instead of moist and keep the area around the dishes neat. Keep litter boxes and pet beds clean and odor free. Pet toys should also be put away. Any damage done to the home by a pet needs to be repaired. You may think the chew marks on the banister are cute but your buyer will not.

Smoking:

Quit. The hard truth is that every cigar or cigarette will cost you money, if not the entire sale. If there have been smokers in the home you will have to make changes or risk not selling the home at all. Many customers are so sensitive to smoke they will not even enter the home that has a whiff of smoke.

From the moment you decide to sell the home smoking inside AND outside the home ceases. No matter how carefully you try to restrict the smoking to the porch or patio, the scent will come back in.

First of all, have the heating and air conditioning systems serviced by a professional. Replace air filters and if necessary have the ductwork cleaned out.

Cigarette smells linger in closets on smoker's and non-smoker's clothes. All clothing and bedding in the home will need to be freshly laundered to get rid of absorbed odors.

Carpets must be replaced or professionally cleaned by a company skilled in removing smoke and nicotine stains.

Repainting the entire home inside, including trim and ceilings, may be required to remove lingering odors. Have several non-smoking friends who will be honest with you walk through your home and give their opinions.

If you are not prepared to do all of these things then assume it will take longer to sell and you will sell your home for less than it is otherwise worth. You will be narrowing your search to that small percentage of buyers who smoke.

Make It Perfect

Fix it:

If it's broken, fix it. If it's damaged, replace it. Your buyer will pay a reasonable price for a home they can move right into. They will pay far less for a "fixer-upper". Buyers who look for fixer-uppers in a down market are looking to "steal" the home for a huge reduction in price.

Most buyers will insist on the contract being contingent on a home inspection by a licensed professional. A thorough home inspection will reveal GFI outlets that don't shut off properly, a back burner on a stove that is broken, a leaky shower head, wood rot by the garage door, and a host of other things both large and small.

Do your own home inspection and go through the property room by room. Then go outside and look at things like lighting, hose bibs, etc. Overlook nothing. If necessary, hire your own home inspection company to check everything out and fix whatever ends up on their list. Then have a "re-inspect" done to get a clean bill of health you can display to prospective buyers.

Being able to display a current inspection that shows no defects may encourage a customer to write a contract on your home instead of the one down the street.

Warranties:

Would you like to have a "health insurance policy" on your home? Then anything that goes wrong would be fixed and you could assure your buyer that they are covered for unexpected problems in the future. There are home warranty companies that do just that.

Obviously, they are not in business to cover "pre-existing" conditions so you'll still have to fix what's wrong now. A good warranty will cover the home while it's on the market, cover many items that come up on an inspection report, and cover the buyer for a period of time after the sale.

Warranties may be different from state to state and company to company. There are variables as to what is covered, the cost involved, and whether you pay up front or at the time the home sells and closes.

A home warranty can reassure a prospective buyer of your home's future condition and make your home look more appealing than the competition. Many real estate agents offer them through their company so check your options before deciding on one.

The small stuff:

Make sure the home is kept the appropriate temperature for the season. A too hot or too cold home will turn off customers and they will spend less time in the home.

Homes should not have strong noticeable smells. Cleaning products should not leave a heavy smell. However, don't go to the other extreme and put too many scented candles and potpourri bowls everywhere. Some of your customers may have allergies and strong smells (even pleasant ones) can work against you.

Vacant homes:

If you must leave your home vacant while it's on the market there are several things you should keep in mind. For one thing, flaws are more obvious in a vacant home. Paint that was retouched or has faded is more apparent. Carpet stains, wear and tear, etc. look more obvious.

It may be necessary to repaint the entire house or whole rooms. In order for the home to look its best, it is a must to have the floor coverings professionally cleaned.

Homes look lifeless when no one lives there so it will be harder for your customers to feel any emotion about the home. So it is important that you leave, or add a few things to brighten it up and add warmth.

In the kitchen, new hand towels and pot holders will add color. A canister set and a couple of cookbooks will make it appear homier.

In the bathroom, fresh towels and a new bath mat will make the room look more appealing. A candle in a nice holder, a small basket of potpourri, or other accessories, will enhance the appeal.

A few nice artificial plants throughout the home can be effective as well. Get ideas from model homes that decorate on a limited budget and you'll come up with a plan. Beware of leaving art work behind. It may or may not help the room's appearance. Use some objective advice from a friend whose taste you admire when considering this.

There are professional stagers that will rent accessories and pieces of furniture to make a vacant home more appealing. Again, check out prices and see examples of their work before making a decision.

Challenge #2 – Pricing

Price It Correctly

Pricing your home correctly is critical any time but even more so in a down market. Overprice it and you miss what would be interested buyers. Underprice it and you lose money. Just like the third little bear, you want to price it "just right". That will take some effort.

Here is how pricing works in different markets:

- In a *seller's market* there is a very limited inventory of homes for sale. No matter at what price you market your home, it will be seen by potential buyers because there are so few homes competing against it. It may or may not sell at that price, but it will be seen by most buyers.

- In a *normal market* you can still be somewhat over-priced and there is a good chance your home will be viewed by many potential customers because the inventory of homes in competition with yours is still somewhat limited.

- In a *down market (or buyer's market),* the deck is stacked against you. There can be dozens of homes that are virtually interchangeable with yours that a potential buyer can view. If you go beyond your immediate area there could even be hundreds. There are well-priced homes in a down market that do not get showings. There are simply too many homes to choose from. In this kind of market, as time passes, even more homes may get added to the inventory. Homes that are priced too high will be ignored in favor of homes that appear to be the best values.

When there are too many homes to investigate, the first thing buyers will do is narrow the search by price range. Being overpriced by even 5 or 10 percent can eliminate your home for many prospective buyers and they will never know you exist. They won't notice that you have nicer features or that your price is negotiable. You are invisible to them.

Market Price

So how do you arrive at a market price? First let's examine "market price". Market price *isn't* what you paid for the home. It *isn't* what you need to sell it for in order to buy your next home. It *isn't* what it will take to pay off the mortgage and the home equity loan and the home improvement loans. It *isn't* what the home down the street sold for last year.

It *is* what a buyer is willing to pay for your home right now. It is that simple. That may not seem fair, but this isn't school recess – it's business. If you have had your home on the market for some time and you have received several offers that are 10% below what you thought your home was worth, then your home is probably worth 10% less than what you had planned. That is an example of market value.

Market value is based on what other homes are selling for, have recently sold for, and the needs and values of the buyers in the market at this point in time. Features that you paid a premium price for in the past may not be in demand now and may not earn back their costs.

For most people the determining factors in a home's worth are square footage and location, neither of which you can control. If the quiet subdivision you bought into now backs up to a busy thoroughfare, your location value may have decreased. Traffic, crime, school districts, commercial activity, etc. all make location value a moving target. Your home may have gone up or down in value because of one of those variables.

Another factor most people fail to realize is that you can also be overbuilt for your market. The largest, nicest home may not sell for a proportionally larger price. Many people would rather pay less for a home and then spend the money to redo it they way they want it done, perhaps in a more moderate manner than you have done.

In a down market you may also be competing with homes in foreclosure. Surveys have proven that for every foreclosed home within your area the value of your home is reduced by 1% or more.

That is why pricing your home properly to begin with is imperative. You can't afford to wait while other homes may have an increasingly negative impact on your home's value.

Where to begin

Get on the computer for your local tax records. Most communities have this information online. You need to pull up the records for your subdivision.

1 – Write down the total number of homes shown for your neighborhood. Be sure not to count parcels owned by the association for common areas or vacant lots. If your neighborhood includes both condos and houses, only count the number of homes in your category.

2 – Check out the dates of the properties sold and write down the number sold in the last twelve months (again, just in your category). By using the tax records you will see ALL the homes sold, not just the ones sold through real estate agents.

The number sold divided by the total number of homes is the turnover rate for the neighborhood. Looking at this number by year will tell you what the turnover rate is each year and you can see what trends are occurring in your area.

3 – Look at the details of the properties that sold recently and note the square footage, the year built, the lot size (if there are different sizes in your area), and any other distinguishing features, such as swimming pools, that are noted in the records. This is information you will use when determining the value of your home.

4 – Drive around the neighborhood and count the for sale signs. You can now calculate the "absorption rate" for your subdivision.

For example, if you learned from the tax records that 15 homes sold in the past twelve months, and there are 30 homes currently on the market, then there is a two year supply of homes on the market right now. So it will take 24 months for the market to absorb all those homes if nothing changes and no new homes are listed.

Unless you can wait up to two years to sell your home, you'll need to price it to be among the next group of homes that will sell.

One of the best strategies a seller can use in pricing the home is to visit all the other homes for sale in the area. Most of them will have an Open House from time to time, so that's a perfect time to check them out. Others may have fliers out front for passers-by to pick up.

This will help in comparing your home with its competition. You'll see their good and bad points and get an idea of what features will be advantages for your home.

Per Square Foot Pricing:

If all the homes in the neighborhood were built within a few years of each other, by the same builder (or similar ones), and there is not a significant difference in the lots (size, location, or view), then you can use a "per square foot" price to start with.

Divide the sales price by the living area square footage (that's the heated and air conditioned space) and you'll have a "per square foot" price. Do that for several of the homes sold in the past twelve months to see if the price per square foot is similar.

Let's assume that a home sold for $200,000 and it was 2000 square feet. Then the per square foot price is $100 per square foot.

Larger homes may be slightly less per square foot and smaller homes may be slightly higher if other factors are similar. This is because the cost of items like heating and air conditioning units and bathrooms don't increase or decrease proportionately with size.

Multiple the average per square foot price by your living area square footage and you have a beginning.

Using that same example, if your home is 2400 square feet, at $100 per square foot, then the starting point for your home is $240,000.

Now you need to make adjustments, just as an appraiser would. Swimming pools, hot tubs, fireplaces, larger or smaller garages, etc. will make your property worth more or less. Even the view from your backyard or location in the community can be important.

Don't expect there to be a formula for those calculations. What a swimming pool or fireplace is worth in a neighborhood of $200,000 homes is not the same as in an area of $500,000 homes.

In an area of older homes, things like a newer roof or a new heater or air conditioner are also valid adjustments. Upgraded kitchens and bathrooms, new floor coverings, fences, etc. may make a home sell faster but they may not sell for more in a down market. According to most national studies, very few improvements earn back what they cost, so don't give your home too big an adjustment for those added features.

Quartile Pricing:

In a buyer's market people tend to look at the least expensive homes in an area. So make a spread sheet of all the homes for sale in your neighborhood. Eliminate the ones substantially larger or smaller and keep the ones similar in size to yours on the list. Take the remaining number and divide it by 4, so that the homes are now in four quartiles, from the least expensive on the bottom to the most expensive on the top.

If you want to sell quickly or be among the next few sales, you'll need to be in the bottom quartile to ensure that your home is seen by potential buyers. Otherwise, buyers may look at the least expensive homes and make a decision without ever seeing yours.

Be sure to go back and look at smaller homes as well and see how they are priced. If your price puts you priced in their range you'll also pick up those buyers who will see your home as a great value when they realize they can get more home for the same amount of money as a smaller one.

If you are in less of a hurry you may choose to be in the next lowest quartile, but you will have fewer showings and typically take longer to sell.

Top 10 Mistakes in Pricing:

1) The most common mistake is listing the home too high in order to *"test the market"*. Peak showing time for a new listing is in the first 30 days. If you miss that window before reducing your price to what the market indicates is reasonable, you have missed buyers and now your home looks less desired.

Worse, in a declining market, the seller who lists too high finds that in the first 30-60 days prices may drop further. Now instead of being moderately too high, he is way over-priced. He is now *"chasing the market"*. The seller then takes a huge price reduction and the market responds by assuming that either he is desperate or that there is something wrong with the home.

2) Don't price your home in league with larger homes or ones with more features. The other problem with over-pricing is that it attracts buyers with the wrong expectations. Your home will now be compared to homes in a price range that offer more features or square footage than yours. Buyers who might be interested in your home won't know it's there because they aren't looking in that price range.

3) Don't base your price completely on the homes currently on the market. Remember that the homes on the market HAVE NOT SOLD. So pricing your home according to what other sellers HOPE to sell for may not be a good strategy. Be sure to look at the most RECENT sales in your area.

4) Many sellers don't look outside their immediate neighborhood. Sellers forget that there are other neighborhoods that are similar to theirs that to an outsider are just as appealing. Those homes are also "competition". Buyers may be willing to drive a bit farther in order to save a substantial amount on the price or to get more home for the same price as yours.

5) Don't ignore the time of year in your market. Some areas sell best when school is out or about to be out. Other areas have other "hot" seasons. If you are trying to sell when your market is notoriously even slower than normal, you may have to make your price even more appealing to get the attention of the few buyers out there.

6) Don't discount the effect of mortgage rates. Even a slight uptick in rates means your customer can afford less than before and some customers were just eliminated from being able to buy your home. So watch rates and make adjustments downward in price if interest rates are trending upward.

7) Don't offer incentives instead of pricing correctly. Many sellers believe that offering to pay closing costs or pre-pay association fees or even offering a bonus to the selling agent will make their home sell faster. While any of those things may help, they don't replace the importance of pricing the home properly to begin with. Again, overpricing means fewer showings so a buyer may not even learn about your offers because they eliminated it on price.

8) Don't price your home based on what your next home will cost you. By that same logic your home might be worth less because the buyer's previous home sold for less. The market is the market. On the plus side, remember that if your current home is worth less, then your "dream" home may also be worth less and it will balance out.

9) Don't base your price on what you think your neighbors will think. Some people feel they "owe" it to their neighbors to keep prices up in the area. You are making a business decision so keep it business. Assume your neighbors would do the same thing.

10) Don't forget to calculate your carrying costs. You probably have a mortgage, homeowners' insurance, property taxes, association fees, and upkeep each month. Every month your home remains on the market you are spending that money. An extra six months on the market can be expensive. It may be better to accept a lower price now than gamble on a higher price later while absorbing carrying costs for an extended period.

Appraisals:

Should you get one? Maybe. If nothing has sold in your area for over six months or your home is unique to the area, then it could be a good idea in order to give you a starting point.

You certainly can't price your home *over* the appraised value. Even if you find a buyer at that price, the home will not appraise for the sales price and the buyer won't get their mortgage. Then you must begin again to find a new buyer because the first buyer will more than likely walk away from the transaction or demand a much lower price.

Appraised value is based on historic data and may not reflect the current market. Homes that sold for $250,000 six months ago may be similar to yours. However, if the inventory now is such that the absorption rate is a year or more, your home may have to be listed for less in order to attract a buyer.

Do You HAVE to Sell? - Other Choices

Before making any decisions on selling your home, evaluate all your options. If you are able to ride out the down market you may be better off waiting to sell in a year or two or more.

Do some number crunching to see if the cash drain you have in the short term is off-set enough by a potential gain in the long term. If the long term gain looks doubtful, then better to cut your losses and sell now. If you can *realistically* see healthy appreciation by waiting, then try to find a way to survive until then.

Renting:

If moving is required and you HAVE to go now, look at the possibility of renting out your home. That isn't a great option because there are risks and costs associated with renting.

One thing to consider is that if you aren't going to be local then you'll need to hire someone to handle the rental for you. That might cost you 10-15% of the total rental income but it's worth it to know that someone is monitoring your property.

Be sure to look at the rental listing agreement and get all the details up front before signing. Some agreements are only for finding the tenant and negotiating the lease. Others include rent collection and property management. Some agreements are negotiable and others are not. If you are not entirely comfortable reviewing an agreement consult your own attorney for advice.

Rentals also carry a certain risk because of potential tenant damage. Is the income worth it if you have to replace the carpet and make repairs in a year? Don't forget to allow for a period of unexpected vacancy when calculating your costs. Tenants are unpredictable, even with a lease.

Your insurance costs will go up with a tenant-occupied home and your property taxes may increase as well. Find out the answers to all those possibilities before deciding.

Do the math and see if the rental amount will cover your mortgage and other expenses. If so, renting may be a valid option. If not, see if you can handle the deficit comfortably. Consider the financial and emotional stress involved as well before you make your final decision.

Financial Problems:

In addition to considering what you owe on the home and any home equity loans you may have, you need to look at what your closing costs will be. Depending on the area of the country, you may be expected to pay several sizable fees when the home sells. Those need to be calculated and added to your mortgage amounts to see if the price you can sell for will pay off all those fees as well as your mortgage debts.

If you are "upside down" on pricing you may owe more on the home that you will be able to sell for. Before putting the home on the market it's time to have a talk with your lender and see what your options are. Walking away with cash in your pocket will probably not be one of them.

Many people have heard the term "short sale". That means the lender will allow you to sell the home for less than is owed. While that may sound like a dream come true, there are conditions.

First of all, the lender may or may not allow it at all, depending on circumstances. Next, the lender will not tell you what price they will accept until you get a contract on the home. The lender may expect you to pay back the difference. You may be taxed on the difference as "ordinary income".

Finally, finding a buyer for a short sale is not easy. Lenders can take months to make a decision on the contract and during that time many buyers walk away, leaving the seller to begin all over again.

Short sales, deed in lieu of foreclosure, bankruptcy, and foreclosure all are potential solutions and all come with consequences. Some are more damaging and long term than others.

Don't make any decisions until you have investigated all your choices. You may also need to seek the advice of an attorney and a tax advisor before making a final decision. Lenders don't want to foreclose and will try to work with you if you make the effort to come up with a workable plan with them.

A word of caution: in a market in which some sellers are desperate to sell their homes and have serious financial problems, there are people out there who will try to take advantage of the situation. If a company contacts you, unsolicited, beware. Your name was on a list and they are looking for an opportunity to make money off your dilemma.

If you don't have an attorney of your own, look for legal aid in the phone book. Talk to your lender. Consult with a not for profit credit counseling service. And don't ever sign over your title to anyone who approaches you with that as a part of the "fix" they are offering.

Challenge #3 — Make Sure It Gets Seen

Exposure to the Market

Now it's time to put the home on the market. You've done your homework and priced it right. You've worked on the home so that it shows at its best. So how do you reach the buyers out there and expose your home to them?

Your home has to be in as many places as possible that buyers might see it. That could include driving by the home, the newspaper, magazines, TV, and the internet. The more people who are exposed to the home, the more likely you'll find the right buyer.

Imagine you had a car for sale. If you just parked it in your driveway with a sign in the window, you would only reach those people who drive past your home. If you parked it at the entrance to your neighborhood you would reach a few more. If you parked it at a local shopping center you would reach even more. If you ran an ad in the newspaper under "Cars For Sale" you would hit people from all over who were specifically looking for a car. Add to that other car-selling publications and websites and you get the point.

If you sell the home yourself, without an agent, you will have difficulty using some of the same resources open to agents. However, because it is your own home you can choose to advertise in places an agent may not because you are setting your own budget.

First, let's look at the team you line up to support you. Then we'll identify the common types of exposure available for your home. Finally, we'll discuss the pros and cons of selling it yourself vs. using an agent.

The team behind you

Whether or not you sell your home yourself or use an agent there are several professionals you may want to consider up front to add to your "team".

Appraiser: Let's start with an appraiser. Real estate agents help their customers find homes in a price range and back it up with "Competitive (or Comparative) Market Analyses". You can confirm that analysis by having a current appraisal done by a certified appraiser. As we stated earlier, you may not sell the home for as much as the appraisal in a down market. However, having a current appraisal to show a potential buyer reassures them that the price they are considering offering is in line with the value.

Home Inspection Company: It isn't a bad idea to go ahead and have a full home inspection done. A good home inspector will find things you don't think of as issues or are even aware of. Then when you have those things repaired you get a re-inspect to show your customers, demonstrating that the property is in good repair.

Home Warranty: A home warranty makes your home competitive with newer homes that are less likely to require repairs in the first few years. Investigate home warranty companies who do business in your state and see what is available to you.

You may find that for a nominal cost you can have both seller and buyer coverage. Seller coverage means things that break while the home is on the market are also covered in the plan. Usually you have to have purchased the buyer coverage in order to get seller coverage but check because it varies by state.

Many real estate companies offer home warranties so if you are using an agent that may be a service they can offer you. If not, check around to see what your choices are.

Attorney or Title Company: Depending on customs in your part of the country it may be common for title companies to handle the closing of escrow or in your area it may be that everyone uses attorneys.

You can consult with the appropriate entity to prepare a preliminary HUD statement that shows both your net proceeds as well as the buyer's closing costs. This will add to your level of confidence that the numbers quoted to you by an agent as to what your net proceeds will be is an accurate estimate.

Lender: If your buyer comes to the home without a real estate agent they may be uninformed as to what is necessary to "bring to the table" in order to buy your home. Having a lender who can create a flier for you showing various scenarios for buyers may be helpful.

For example, the flier might show the purchase price, down payment, mortgage amount, interest rate, principle and interest payment, etc. He can include examples with different down payments or using different types of mortgages. Either you or a listing agent can request this.

How to expose your home to the market

There are many avenues available with which to market your home. Some are more effective than others. Some cost more than others. In a tough market it's important not to overlook any option or do a half-way job on it.

Signage:

The most basic place to begin is with the sign. Unless your neighborhood has special sign restrictions there will be a sign in front of your home. It will have either the agent's contact information or yours. If your home isn't easily found by the casual driver, you may also want to consider some directional signs to place in the neighborhood.

Open Houses:

Are they necessary? Real estate agents will tell you that the national statistics show a less than 2% chance of selling a home through an open house. Most agents know this and will advise you on what is best in your market.

However, some homes do sell at an open house and as an owner/seller you shouldn't pass an opportunity by that might work. If you are selling the home yourself you should consider holding an open house on a regular basis.

In most markets Sunday afternoon is the best time for open houses. Check your area and plan to be open when other homes in your area are open. Then you can piggy-back on the traffic they generate.

If there are not a lot of open houses in your area you or your agent should consider running an ad for those days to promote it. Most local newspapers have a section just for open houses.

Make sure there is an Open House sign and also directional signs in the area pointing toward your home. If you are located on a heavily trafficked street you may not need the directional signs.

You need to make sure the home looks good and smells good for an open house. Experts suggest you bake cookies or a cake to make the home smell appealing. The most important thing is that the home feels inviting.

Turn off the TV and turn on soft music. Banish the family and pets. No one should be home for this but you or the agent (Not both. Sellers should never be present if an agent is holding the open house.)

There should be information to hand out and copies of surveys, appraisals, home inspections, etc. to show if required.

Don't be surprised if no one shows up or if the customers who do come, all arrive at the same time. Agents have to deal with this too. Open houses are just unpredictable.

Fliers:

In many areas, homes for sale have an information box near the sign with fliers about the home inside. If this is common in your area then you should have one as well. Make sure there are always fliers in the box, so if the home is vacant be sure to check on it frequently.

If you are selling the home yourself you will be creating the fliers. If you have listed the home you agent will handle that. Either way, there are guidelines for really good fliers.

First of all they should be printed on a heavier stock paper than copy paper, and in color. The flier should have an easy to read font, photos that show off the home to its best advantage, and they should point out features that set the home apart.

The flier should not include *everything* there is to know about the home. The flier is a teaser when it's in the flier box to make the customer want to see inside and know more. Once they are inside it's a guide that highlights and explains what makes the home special.

If there is important information the customer should have that can't be included on the flier, have a notebook to put inside the home in a prominent place. That notebook can include a copy of a recent appraisal, a current home inspection report, a floor plan, a survey, etc. Never include originals in this, only copies, just in case someone thinks it's for them to take home. To avoid any confusion, add a note that states that copies are available upon request.

Newspaper Advertising:

Nearly every town in America has a daily newspaper. If you are listing the home with an agent, find out how often and in what format your home will be advertised. You may appear in the company ad on a rotating basis or your agent may place classified ads for just your home. Make sure the agent is specific on what he has planned.

If you are selling the home yourself find out from the advertising department which days have the highest readership and in which sections. You will probably want to advertise in the classified section in your area from time to time and also in the open house section on those days. Running larger "display" ads on your own is probably not cost-effective but you should price them before you decide.

There are also typically smaller newspapers in most areas that cover a particular niche market. It might focus on your part of town, or something else. Check them out and see what their real estate section looks like. It might target your buyer and be a good place to promote your home. While it may not replace the daily newspaper it could expose your home to a group of readers who might miss it otherwise. This is an opportunity open to you or an agent.

Magazines:

There are many real estate magazines out there. Some agents advertise in certain publications but this is a very market specific activity and not as productive in some parts of the country as others.

Most home magazines will not sell advertising to "For Sale by Owners", but if that's the case don't worry about it. Buyers use those magazines to supplement their other searches, not as their only means of finding a home, so you will have a chance to be seen elsewhere.

Television:

In many markets there is a real estate channel through the local cable company. Some only sell to real estate agents and others allow owners to advertise their homes. You or your agent can include this in a marketing plan if it appears to be effective in your area.

Check out the pricing and number of viewers (the channel's advertising department can tell you). Depending on the cost and number of times your ad would be seen it may or may not be a good idea.

MLS:

The "Multiple Listing Service" is the biggest method by which your home will be found for two reasons. First, most homes are sold by real estate agents and that is where your home must be in order to be found by agents. The second reason is because it overlaps the internet. Many property search websites draw their information from the local MLS's around the country.

Here is where it gets challenging. If you are listed with a real estate agent, your home will be on the MLS and therefore in many internet searches. However, the courts have upheld the right of MLS's across the country to restrict listings to members, meaning other brokers. So you don't have access to it unless you hire a broker. Not being in the MLS in your area will effectively eliminate you from many of the most prominent real estate websites in the country.

Virtual Tour:

This is a feature most agents offer and one you should insist on if you are listing your home with an agent. Customers expect to be able to view the home online prior to calling for a showing. Also, many websites rank homes with virtual tours higher in their searches, making a home without one harder to find. Good virtual tours may include panoramic shots of the exterior and possibly interior, various photos of the main living areas, and sometimes even photos of the community amenities.

Internet:

There is nothing more important for sellers than exposure on the internet. Conservative estimates show that over 80% of home buyers begin their search for a home on the internet these days.

However, there is no one place to go that shows a potential buyer EVERYTHING for sale in a given market. There is not a website that will include ALL the listings of agents and ALL of the For Sale by Owner listings on the same website.

There are national, well-known websites for searches of homes listed through MLS systems. Most that have national prominence are set up that way. They can instantly access new listings and update changes as they occur.

There is a lot of money spent by those sites to get customers' attention and they do work. To be included on those you must be listed with an agent or a company that offers that listing for a fee. There is no other way.

A word about Ad Copy

No matter whether the words appear in a newspaper ad or on a flier, the point is to stimulate interest in the home for a potential buyer. You want to make the phone ring.

Use the space you have to describe what makes your home special. If the home has a spectacular back yard that sets it apart from other homes, feature that. Don't spend time on the features that are the same as competing homes. Think "lifestyle". What is it about your home that gives it a lifestyle your buyer might want?

If you are selling the home yourself and aren't sure about what to say, spend time looking at other ads for homes. See what appeals to you that was said in the ad. Craft ads and fliers that allow a buyer to see what is exceptional about your home.

What else:

To properly expose the home to the market it must be easily accessible. That means a customer needs to be able to reach someone 7 days a week at just about any time to arrange a showing.

Agents who might want to show the home must be able to reach whoever is in charge of the appointments and must be able to have someone to let them in or be able to have a key available.

If you are selling it yourself then make sure you can be reached at work or home any time someone inquires. You will need to be available to show it at all hours on any day.

If you are listing with an agent, make sure their office is open seven days a week or that the agent is on call for buyer inquiries at all times.

If you have pets, be sure that they are either out of the home or out of the way, for showings. Many buyers will not go into a home with an uncaged dog. You don't want to miss a showing that may not come again because no one was available to walk the dog.

In a down market there can be no stone left unturned to expose the home to as many potential buyers as possible if you are to find the right one.

Selling it yourself

Unfortunately, while sellers want to save the commission, so do buyers. A seller believes he can price his home at a price equivalent to homes marketed through agents and therefore save the difference. The potential buyer knows that and realizes there is more negotiating room because of that difference. Both parties want to save the same money. It can't be done.

Or the seller prices the home at a price he believes will be advantageous because he's already deducted the commission. The buyer still believes there is negotiating room AND he may believe that the seller is desperate because of the lower than market price.

The seller can end up selling it himself with a net price the same as if he had used an agent, plus he did all the work. Don't forget to budget for the marketing you must do to successful expose your home to potential buyers and the value of your time when figuring out your net proceeds.

This is NOT to say it can't be done, and done successfully. It's just that in a down market it is more difficult and challenging for the seller.

Remember, whether you are listed with an agent or not, from now on your home must stay neat and clean, 24/7 (or close to it).

How to handle real estate agents:

You are going to be besieged with calls from agents who would like to list your home. Now is the time to strategize on how you will handle those calls.

They will be calling with two types of requests and you need to have an answer to each one. If they are calling to list your home, decide how long you will try it on your own before you consider listing and tell them to check back in (blank) amount of time. If they are calling to see if you will pay a commission if they bring a buyer, have an answer as to whether or not you will pay and how much you will pay.

It's in your best interest to say you will agree to a commission if they bring a buyer and the expected fee is usually half of what the fee would have been if you listed with them. The logic is that you are doing all the marketing and showings so you are the "listing" side of the transaction and they, since they have the buyer, are the "selling" side.

You are not obligated to pay the commission unless they bring you a buyer with an acceptable contract. The fee will be included on the contract so you can calculate your net proceeds from the sale before you decide whether or not to sign. Then the commission will be deducted from your net proceeds at closing.

If you have the luxury of time to try to sell it yourself before you decide to list the home with an agent, this can be a way of researching potential agents. The ones who call you one time and then go away, never to be heard from again, may not be people you'd want to hire. The agents who follow up in a professional way during the time you are selling it yourself should be considered if and when you decide to use a real estate agent.

If an agent calls you repeatedly and always just asks you the same questions and offers no comments, that tells you something. If an agent follows up and offers suggestions or asks incisive questions, you have learned something about them that may be worth considering down the road.

Make notes on who calls, and what is said. Keep any mailings or notes, as well as business cards. Should you end up deciding to list with an agent, you'll have a starting point to decide which ones you might prefer to investigate further and which ones you can eliminate.

Agent Showings:

If you have allowed an agent to show your home, you should be there to let them in. Do NOT leave a key for them unless you have met them and verified them to be who they say they are. You should call the office directly to be sure their license is current and they are still associated with that company. There are people out there who prey upon what they perceive to be vulnerable sellers.

Meet the agent and customer at the door, invite them to look around, tell them you'll be outside if they have any questions, then leave. Go rake the yard, or feed the birds, or sit in the tree house. Just get out of the way. If you hover, the customer won't feel comfortable to explore on their own or make comments to their agent.

You should NOT guide them around and point out things. The agent is a professional and they know how to show a home. If they have questions, they will find you and ask. As they leave, thank them for coming and offer to answer any questions they might think of later. DO NOT ask them for an opinion at that moment.

If it was a productive showing and the home fits the needs of the customer you will get a call from the agent. If it did not fit, for whatever reason, you will probably not get a call. Don't expect a lot of feedback from the agent because you did not hire them and they will feel no loyalty to you at this point.

Your own showings:

Most people will call to make an appointment to see your home. A few may show up on your doorstep and ask to see it immediately. Politely refuse and set up a better time. Take their name and phone number in case something changes. Serious buyers will be respectful of that and be accommodating.

"Looky-loos" who are just out there "playing" may be impatient and pushy. Don't feel you have to show your home to everyone who calls or comes by or at any hour. It is still *your* home.

You should consider asking a number of questions of a potential buyer before you agree to set an appointment with them. An agent does this to determine if a buyer is "ready, willing, and able" to make a buying decision.

What you don't want to do is waste your time on someone who is not financially qualified, who doesn't plan on buying for a year, or who has unrealistic expectations of your home or needs your home can't meet.

Taking the time to ask the questions up front will save you time in the long run. Agents typically have a list of questions they use with any potential buyer to ensure they don't waste their own or their seller's time with inappropriate showings.

Here is a form you can use to screen prospective customers. Remember that a customer who refuses to give out any information is probably not a serious buyer. Every question is important to determine how serious the buyer is, their timetable for buying, the appropriateness of your home for them, and their financial qualifications. Make copies so that you can use one for each buyer you interview.

Buyer Prospect Interview   Date_____

Name _____

Address _____ City _____

State _____ Zip _____

Phone _____ _____ _____
            Home   Cell   Email

Why are you buying/moving? _____

Will you be buying for: _____ Primary _____ Vacation Home
_____ Investment

Do you currently..... Own _____?

      Do you need to sell your home before you can buy? _____
      _____

      Is it on the market now? _____

      How long has it been on the market? _____

      Is it under contract, and if so when will it close? _____
      _____

Do you currently........   Rent _____?

      When is your lease up? _____

      Can you be released early?_ _____

Is this a scouting time for you, or do you plan to purchase at this time?_____

If not now, what is your target date? _____

_____

How long have you been looking? _____

Why haven't you bought yet? _____

Are you working with an agent? _____ Who? _____

_____

Why are you interested in this area? _____

_____

What is it about this home that appealed to you? _____

_____

How many: bedrooms _____, baths _____,
do you need? Square footage? _____

What is your price range? _____

_____

Do you plan to finance? _____

Are you already working with a lender? _____

Have you been pre-approved? _____

Appointment Date & Time _____

Showing the home:

Ideally you should have any customers who visit sign a registration form. This way you can follow up later. However, many people are uncomfortable with signing in because they don't want to be "bugged" later. Don't be surprised if those people who reluctantly sign in use a fictitious name or phone number.

When a buyer shows up for an appointment greet them at the door and give them your flier. Escort them through the home, but don't lead them. Direct them, then follow. Allowing them to enter a room first gives a better impression.

Point out features that are not visible or obvious. For example, you might mention that the new appliances are all energy efficient, or that the carpet has a 10 year warranty, or that you get great sunsets from the lanai. Don't say the rooms are big, or there is plenty of closet space, or "this is the kitchen". Buyers can figure out those things for themselves.

Don't allow the buyers too much privacy but again, don't hover. Invite them to ask questions and then give concise answers. Too many sellers oversell the home and scare off potential buyers without meaning to.

As they are leaving, thank them for considering your home. Offer to answer any questions later if they want to call back. Don't put them on the spot and ask if they are interested in your home. Even if they are interested they may have to talk about it first with each other before they feel comfortable letting you know.

Safety tips:

In most states a brand new real estate agent is given a short course on safety because there have been incidents in which agents have been attacked or robbed while showing a home or conducting an open house. Being a For Sale By Owner also exposes you to a certain amount of risk.

Most of the people you will encounter in selling your home are only interested in you and your home as customers. However, the potential is there for someone who has other intentions to take advantage of the access and privacy you give them. Without trying to scare you there are some tips you should know about.

You should never set an appointment for a showing unless you get a name and phone number first. Then call the number back to confirm the appointment and to see that the number does work. Then give that information to a friend who will call you back after the showing to confirm your safety.

That same friend should be aware of every showing appointment you make and should check in afterwards with you. If your friend is a neighbor, that person can also walk outside and take down the license number of the car. That way if anything does happen or property goes missing, you have both a phone number and a description of the vehicle to give the police.

Never let anyone in without an appointment except during an open house. Even if a real estate agent shows up, do not allow them in without at least getting a business card and then calling the office number on it to verify they do, in fact, work there. Describe the person (if there is no photo on the card) just to make sure you are dealing with someone who is who he represents himself to be.

As stated earlier, valuables should already be removed from the home. During a showing your purse should be well hidden as well. Don't be afraid to enlist a friend to help you with an open house.

Never lead anyone into a room. Always let them go in and *then* you go in so they can't block the door. Stay with the customer and keep aware of where they are and where you are in relation to exits.

After someone has been in your home, go back and make sure all windows and doors are secured.

Using common sense and being careful not to take unnecessary risks is the smart way to operate while your home is on the market.

Marketing the home yourself

Everything you'd expect from an agent you'll need to do yourself. However, there are some differences and tips to keep in mind.

Signs:

Don't go to the home improvement store and buy the red on white "For Sale By Owner" sign. You will have made a lousy first impression to your potential customers. They see "cheap sign" and think "cheap house".

There are local sign companies, as well as sign companies online, that offer inexpensive, custom made signs. Have one made that says your home is for sale and has a phone number you will answer at any hour of the day or night. You do NOT need to say "by owner". It will be obvious that you are selling it by owner since there is no broker name listed.

You will also need nice looking open house signs so have everything made at the same time. Don't forget to buy directional signs if you home is off the beaten path.

Yes, this is a little more expensive than the ready-made signs, but if you want your customers to believe your home is as nice as other homes on the market then your marketing must appear to be as professionally done.

Flier Box:

Be sure to get one that is weather-proof. You need to protect the fliers inside from the rain above and sprinkler systems below. Then put about 10 fliers in the box and keep it that way at all times. Too many fliers make it look like no one is interested in the home. Too few and you run the risk of it being empty on the one day the right buyer drove past.

MLS:

There are services out there that are essentially "fee for service" listing companies. They are members of the local board and they will "list" your home for a fee. Those fees can vary dramatically and typically offer just a basic listing that gets you included in the MLS. Anything more elaborate will cost more.

However, this does get you into the MLS where you will be found by agents. You will now be *expected* to offer compensation to an agent who does bring you a buyer and to state what that amount or percentage will be.

(Take a minute to do the math now: half the fee you are trying to save has just been potentially charged to you in addition to the actual listing fee.)

While this does get your home more exposure to the public through those websites, it will not put your home on even standing with other listings in the eyes of real estate agents. Agents recognize that while you are offering a commission, they know that without an agent representing you, that it is much more difficult to make the sale come together and stay together. They also know that they will end up doing the work of two agents all the way till closing. Consequently, they may still avoid showing your home.

Virtual Tour:

If you decide to have your home listed through one of these services make sure you have the option of purchasing a virtual tour of your home. Most of the virtual tour companies are available only through listing brokers, so make sure you have that choice if possible.

Internet:

If you are not in the MLS there are still sites that are just for For Sale By Owners. Unfortunately, none of them are very comprehensive. Before you decide to pay them to list your home, run a test. Put in your zip code or town and see how many homes show up. Compare sites with each other and compare them with the ads you see in the newspaper. Very few of them charge enough to be able to offer you a listing that will be uploaded by any of the national, well-recognized sites.

Because the number of websites and what they offer changes daily you should check out the availability and requirements of each one and promote your home on as many of them as possible. These days the exposure offered on the internet is key to selling a home, whether it is listed with an agent or not.

Finally:

If you plan to sell your home yourself be sure you have considered all the angles. Do you have the time to devote to the marketing and showing activities? Is the amount of money saved worth the time and expense involved? Are you available at any time to show the home? Have you researched and priced out your marketing choices? Do you feel comfortable discussing financial qualifications and other personal information with potential buyers? Are you able to negotiate in a calm and confident manner?

If the answer to all these questions is "yes" then you're ready. Create a plan for marketing and preparing your home for sale. Then go for it!

Selling the Home with a Real Estate Agent

You've decided you want professional help to sell your home. Chances are that once you begin to tell your friends that you are in the market for an agent you'll be overwhelmed with calls and mailings. How do you begin to sort through them all to decide who to interview?

Ask friends and family who they have used in the past and start a list. See if some names come up more often than others.

Drive around your neighborhood and similar neighborhoods and see what name is on the signs. Add those names to your list and see where they overlap.

If you tried to sell your home yourself first, you will have been contacted by a number of agents who have wanted to talk to you about listing your home for sale. Hopefully, you kept those names and made notes as to which ones impressed you on that first contact so you can add their names to the list.

Decide on the ones you'd like to interview and schedule the appointments. Talk to at least two or three but no more than five or six. You need to be able to compare services but don't make it an endless or confusing process.

Have a list of questions prepared so that you can later compare the agents and what they offer. Let the agent go through their presentation as you make notes. If there is anything they did not cover that was on your list, wait until the end of the presentation to bring it up and ask your question.

Here are some of the questions you need to ask. Make copies so that you can have one for each agent you interview.

Questions for a Prospective Listing Agent

1.   What is your marketing plan for my home?   Is it in writing?

2.   What part of the marketing is paid for by your company and what part is paid for by you, the agent?

3.   What websites will be used to promote the home?

4.   How often will you be in touch with me for updates and by what means (email, phone call, letter, or in person)?

5.   Will these updates come from you or an assistant?

6.   What price do you recommend I list the home for and how did you arrive at that price?

7.   What is my "net" result on the sale of my home after expenses?

8.   What commission do you charge and what services do I receive for that?

9.   Will you be using a "lock box" or "key safe" on my home?

10.   How will showings be scheduled? Do outside agents or customers call you or your office or do they call me directly?

11.   What will happen when a contract comes in on my home? How will you present it to me and how are negotiations handled?

Now let's talk about each one on those questions:

1.   What is your marketing plan for my home? Is it in writing?

This needs to be specific and detailed. It should include, at a minimum, a flier for the home, advertising, mailings, and a virtual tour. The advertising plan should include specifics on where it will be advertised and how often, as well as details on the mailings.

Take a look at examples of advertising the agent has done on other listings to see if it looks professionally done or just cheap and basic.

On examples of the flier, look at the wording used to describe the home to see if it made the home sound appealing. Do the photos enhance the best features of the home?

What mailings will the agent do? To whom? How often?

Go online and look at a virtual tour the agent has done on one of his listings. Again, does it make you want to know more about that home or is it just a series of unimaginative photos?

2.   What part of the marketing is paid for by your company and what part is paid for by you, the agent?

This is important because some agents work for "full service" brokers who pay for most of the advertising. Agents who work for "discount" or "limited service" brokers pay for it themselves. In a down market, if an agent is struggling or has too many listings, they may cut out some marketing if they have to pay for it themselves. Another reason to get the marketing plan in writing.

3.   What websites will be used to promote the home?

This is where size can matter. A larger company typically has agreements with more websites that can be used to promote their listings. Be sure to get a list. Then later, look at each website to see what those listings look like and how easy they were to find.

4.   How often will you be in touch with me for updates and by what means (email, phone call, letter, or in person)?

Updates should be weekly and should include not only the showings of your home that week, but what else occurred in the market you are in – new listings, listings that sold, price changes on other homes, etc.

This report should be in writing and is usually done via email. However, there should be a follow-up conversation in person or on the phone periodically to review the details and to discuss what they mean.

For every showing you should be given the feedback your agent received from the other agent or customer who saw your home. Each week you should also receive in writing the specific marketing activities that promoted your property.

5.   Will these updates come from you or an assistant?

A very busy agent may have an assistant who will call you or send you the information. This is not as good as talking to the agent. An assistant usually will not be able to answer questions you may have.

On the other hand, a busy agent is usually a successful one. If the assistant is doing the follow-up, make sure there is a way to easily reach the agent with your questions. Find out how often the agent plans to speak with you personally. Again, get all this in writing.

6.   What price do you recommend I list the home for and how did you arrive at that price?

Most agents prepare a "CMA" or Comparative Market Analysis to see what similar homes in your area have sold for. They will also present you with information about what similar homes are currently selling for.

Using that information they will be able to recommend a price or a narrow price range they feel will be the price at which to list your home. Be sure to look carefully at the homes selected for comparison to be sure that the conclusions drawn seem reasonable.

7.   What is my "net" result on the sale of my home after expenses?

Agents have a "Seller's Net Sheet" that they use to calculate the expenses you will have for the closing, including all the costs that are typically paid by the seller. The agent will know in your area what expenses are considered "usual and customary" for the seller and what costs a buyer may ask a seller to pay in a down market.

After subtracting these costs and the commission for selling the home, as well as any outstanding mortgage amount, the "net" result is what the seller will receive in cash at the closing.

If you have questions about the closing costs, the agent should be comfortable explaining them to you.

8.   What commission do you charge and what services do I receive for that?

Full service brokers will provide you with a comprehensive list of services that include the full marketing program, etc. Discount, or limited service brokers, usually don't offer the same services so they may charge a lower commission. However, agents always have the option of supplementing the marketing their company offers if they feel it's necessary.

(A word on commissions: Companies cannot legally decide together what they will all charge so they do not necessarily charge the same thing. Individual company policies can dictate that their agents charge certain commissions. Each agent you speak to will be able to explain their company's policies.)

Selecting the listing agent who offers the lowest commission as the <u>*primary*</u> *reason for choosing them is never a good idea. Especially in a down market. You really do get what you pay for.*

9.   Will you be using a "lock box" or "key safe" on my home?

With the cost of gas high, and the time involved to go get a key, most agents prefer to use what is known as a "lock box" or "key safe" on your home. The key for the home is inside and an agent who wants to show your home must have a code or special electronic key to open it. Some key safes are able to electronically record who opened it last, so that if a key were missing, it's easy to track down who had it last.

Key safes make it easier for agents to show your home so you should always request one if they are common in your area.

10.   How will showings be scheduled? Do outside agents or customers call you or your office or do they call me directly?

Full service brokers usually staff their phones with a real person, 7 days a week. That way it's easy for an agent to call in and make an appointment to show your home.

If the showing agent has to call your agent to set the appointment there is the risk of playing "phone tag" for hours and the showing agent may just give up and you lose a showing.

Again, the easier it is to show your home, the more likely it is to be shown, and to more people.

11.   What will happen when a contract comes in on my home? How will you present it to me and how are negotiations handled?

Once in awhile a customer will make a verbal offer on your home. Verbal offers cannot legally be enforced and they don't usually include all the terms that would be in a written contract. You can instruct your agent to only accept written offers.

Written offers should be presented to you by your agent and in person. When doing so, they should explain fully both the price and the terms.

Your agent should explain to you how he will present the offers and give you the confidence that you will be able to make intelligent decisions with his guidance.

What NOT to do:

1) Don't list with someone just because they tell you your home will sell for a higher price than someone else says. Even if you plan to list your home with a real estate broker, do your own homework first. Find out your own market data.

Unfortunately, while there are agents (most of them) who do the proper research and present a thorough Competitive Market Analysis, there are others who will want to "buy" your listing. They will agree to whatever price you ask for in order to get the listing.

They are afraid to tell the truth for fear of not getting the listing, or they didn't take the time to understand the current market and your home. List with the agent who presents data they can back up, even if it isn't the news you wanted to hear.

2) Don't list with someone who won't give you a written marketing plan. Plans that are not in writing can be mis-remembered. It also makes it difficult to compare what agents are offering. Those plans should also explain how often they will be in touch with you for follow-up and by what means (email, phone calls, in person, etc.).

If the plan is in writing and the agent you select fails to live up to their written commitment, it's easier to demonstrate that failure if you want to terminate the agreement.

3) Don't just consider agents who have done business before in your area. Many good agents are capable of listing and selling a home in areas new to them and can do it as well as an agent who has sold there before. Agents are constantly educating themselves in the market.

4) Don't assume brand new agents can't sell your home. Sometimes new agents have the skills from other walks of life that make them good marketers or skilled negotiators. New agents may also be "hungrier" to do a good job for you.

5) Don't assume the top agent in the company will give you the best service. That may or may not be true. In-depth questions to past customers should supply the information you need. Ask for references. Apply the same questions and criteria to any agent you are considering.

Other considerations:

How accessible will your agent be?

Ask that question. What hours is the office open? You can easily verify this information by testing it the day following your meeting with the agent. Try to call the agent's phone number and try to contact the agent through the office number. See how quickly you get through and how good the service was.

You can be your own "mystery shopper" by enlisting the help of a friend. Have your friend call on one of the agent's listings and see what happens. How easily did they reach the agent? Or did the agent return the call promptly? Were they enthusiastic about the property and try to get the "customer" to take a look in person? You can learn a lot this way.

How long is the listing agreement and can you cancel early?

Most of the agents will require a similar length of time for the listing agreement so you should expect that whatever is "usual and customary" in your area will be the norm. Take your listing agent's advice there and list for that period of time. It may seem like a long time but in a down market the agent knows what amount of time it may take.

You will only want to cancel the agreement early if your situation changes and you decide not to sell or the agent has not lived up to what was promised. Find out what the cancellation policy is and make sure it is in writing, not just verbal.

What is the reputation of the broker behind the agent?

The company that backs the agent is really who you are listing with. How long have they been in business? If it is a franchise, as many are, how long has that individual franchise been around? Who owns it? What is their background?

This is important because if anything were to come up on your listing, it is the broker behind your agent who will be involved in solving the problem. Some brokers have been in business for decades and have extensive background in real estate. Others bought the franchise or opened their doors recently and have limited experience.

It is just as important that the broker have experience as it is for your agent. The broker is legally responsible for your transaction. What kind of market share does the broker have? That means the percentage of homes in the area that the broker sells. Where is the broker located? These are all factors to consider.

Should you hire a "team"?

Most agents work as individuals. Some work as a team. There are pros and cons to hiring a team. If you are interviewing someone who offers the fact that they have a team as an advantage, ask more questions. Who will I be speaking to for showing feedback? How often will I hear from *my* agent? Does my agent do any of the showings?

References

In spite of what answers you receive there is only one way to find out for sure what it's like to deal with this agent – ask for references and check them. Ask for at least 10 references and check several of them at random.

Ask all the questions you can think of. These people should give you enthusiastic and detailed responses. The most important question you should save for last: *If you or a friend or family member had a home to sell, would you use or recommend this agent again?* Then, *Why or why not?* Listen for the words, any hesitation, etc. to see if you are getting a true endorsement.

Making your decision

You've researched prospective agents, held your interviews, reviewed their materials, mystery shopped them, and checked their references. You've eliminated anyone who didn't measure up on any one of those things. Now what? This is a business decision. Don't choose simply based on a personal relationship or fear of hurting someone's feelings. Your gut instinct should tell you who will be the best and who to choose. Pick that person and get started.

What happens once the home is on the market?

From showing to contract

Your listing agent will go over the details of how your home is to be shown. If you are selling it yourself you've already made those decisions. All the same rules apply as to preparing the home and keeping it neat and clean, whether it is listed with an agent or not.

Your agent will usually recommend, or you will decide, how the appointments are to be handled. Cooperate in the way that will make it easiest to confirm the appointments for agents who want to show your home.

Now comes the hard part – you wait. You wait for showings. You wait for ads to run. You wait for open houses. You wait for a contract.

Showing Feedback

If you are selling the home yourself you'll have instant feedback. Buyers will ask questions if they are interested in your home. A lack of questions usually means a lack of interest. If you listed with an agent you will be getting feedback on the showings that occur.

If any of the feedback is negative you need to deal with it. Perhaps the listing agent was right when he advised you to repaint the kitchen or clean out the garage. Perception is reality and if you hear the same feedback more than once you have to assume it is preventing you from selling the home and you need to decide what to do.

Price Adjustments

If the home is priced right when it was listed and marketed properly you should have showings fairly quickly, even in a down market. If you have not received any showings in the first few weeks then you are priced too high. Homes that are priced even close to the right price will get at least some activity. If yours is not getting showings, you're priced too high.

If you get showings but no offers, you may still be priced a little high. The market is setting the price, as it always does. If it indicates your price is too high it is because there are other homes competing with yours that are perceived as better values.

When it appears that price is an issue don't delay. Drop it immediately and rely on your agent or current data to give you the truth about where the market is for your home. Better to take a reasonable drop in price now and get it sold than to watch the market possibly drop even lower and have to make a much larger adjustment later to get it sold.

You get a contract, now what?

When you are selling the home yourself you will get a call from a buyer who says they would like to make an offer on your home. It may or may not be in writing. If it isn't in writing you should state that you will only consider written offers. This protects you from the "bottom feeder" who is not buying a home, but is only looking for a "steal". They typically offer low prices to sellers until they find one that says "yes". Then they may write it up with terms you would not otherwise agree to. Serious buyers will have no objection to putting their offer in writing.

If you are listed, your agent will call to say you have an offer and to schedule a time to present it to you in person. At that time he will explain both the price and the terms of the offer. Make sure that you review the contract in person. Don't try to make decisions over the phone. It's too easy to overlook the details of the contract that make it good or bad.

A contract is a balance of price and terms and both are important. Both price and terms are negotiable. First we'll discuss the terms of the contract.

The binder deposit

The first term is how much of a binder deposit the buyer has put down, and how much more they intend to make as a down payment.

This will give you an idea of how financially capable the buyer is of buying the home. In many states the binder is all that is at risk if the buyer defaults on the contract so a sizable binder can also indicate the how serious the buyer is about the contract.

Financing

Next is the financing. Are they getting a mortgage or paying cash? How much is the mortgage? Is the contract contingent on the buyer getting approval for the mortgage?

What type of mortgage is it? Some mortgages are more difficult to qualify for than others, meaning you may or may not have a buyer who is capable of completing the purchase. How quickly will they have loan approval? Is the loan approval contingent on something? Are they presenting a pre-approval letter with the contract that shows they have made application already and have a tentative loan approval?

Now is a time to engage the members of your "team". If you are selling it yourself, call the lender you are working with to discuss the financing offered. Or your agent can go over it with you. You want to be sure that it looks reasonable.

Closing costs

What, if any, closing costs is the buyer expecting you to pay that are outside what is considered "usual and customary" in your area? Anything above what you had anticipated will affect your net proceeds in a negative way – you'll make less on the sale.

Many times, particularly in a down market, the buyer will ask the seller to pay the buyer's closing costs and pre-paid items. It accomplishes two things: it lowers the overall cost to the buyer, and it also allows a buyer with limited cash to be able to afford the home.

Don't be surprised by this or disregard an offer just because it includes this term. It may otherwise be a good offer.

Date of closing

When do they plan to close escrow on the home? Does that timetable work with your schedule? In most areas a closing can take place in 30 to 45 days. Again, your mortgage representative or agent can advise you if the closing date on the contract is realistic.

Once you have an accepted contract your home is no longer actively marketed. Other buyers won't usually look at a home that is under contract. So what you don't want to do is have a closing date that is too far in advance.

If something goes wrong and the buyer is unable to close you will have lost valuable time being able to market your home to other buyers. Again, your agent or lender can give you advice here.

Clauses and addendums

Are there any clauses or addendums added to the contract? Are they written properly? Your agent or attorney can advise you if the language is correct and what they mean.

Other contingencies

What other contingencies are in the contract? Is it contingent on the home inspection or any other inspections? How quickly will that take place? Until all contingencies are met, including the financing contingency, you don't really have a firm contract you can depend on.

Remember that everything is negotiable, including the terms. You can accept or counter anything in the contract until both you and the buyer have agreed on everything.

For example, the price may be low but the terms could include a quick closing and state that the buyer is already pre-approved for the mortgage so there is no mortgage contingency. That contract might be superior to one with a higher price that is shaky on financing or closing date.

Period of offer

Most offers include a "period of offer" that states how long the seller has to respond. This does not usually mean this is a "take it or leave it offer". It just means that your response should be timely so that if you reject the offer or counter the price or terms, the process will move along quickly.

Keep in mind that once you change ANYTHING on the contract you have voided the buyer's obligation to the contract and it is now their choice as to accept your changes. They are no longer legally bound by their original offer. Don't nitpick. Only counter price or important terms.

Now let's look at price.

Price

Because the media has trained buyers to believe they can get a home at a fraction of its listed price, don't be surprised if the first offer you receive is a low one. The buyer is not trying to offend you. Buyers may first "test the waters" to see what your response will be.

Try to find out, if you can, something about the buyers. Is this a first-time home buyer? Are they moving from out of town? Are they planning on living in the home or renting it out as an investment? You or your agent may be able to find out this information, and if so, it will give you some insight into what the buyer's plans are.

The buyer who is buying for investment purposes will likely be more concerned about price than anything else. The buyer who is planning on making this property a home is more likely to negotiate.

If you feel the price offered is too low, you have a right to ask how the buyer arrived at that price. Again, the buyer may or may not be willing to share that, but many will.

ALL offers should be taken seriously if they are in writing and have a binder deposit, no matter how low. Discuss each offer with your agent or advisor and decide how to respond. Many times in a down market the first offer on a home is the best one. If prices continue to drop, the offer that looked horribly low today may look desirable in two months.

If you have several contracts submitted over time and all of them are lower than you would consider, you may have to reevaluate your listed price and what you can hope to net. The market may be sending you a message that your home isn't worth what you thought it was.

Negotiations

Some contracts go back and forth several times before everyone is in agreement on price and terms. Others give it one shot and then back out. There is no way to predict how any one buyer will react.

Now is the time to look back at the recent sales history in your area with your agent. Look at the list to sales ratio for other homes. For example, if most homes priced similarly to yours have sold for 95% of list price recently, it's appropriate to shoot for the same result with your home.

However, if nothing has sold recently and there are a number of homes similar to yours for a buyer to choose from, you may be forced to accept a lower offer because it may your only offer.

Try to remain objective in the negotiation process and see the buyer's point of view. Don't take things personally or get emotional, even if you feel the offer is insulting. The buyer is just responding to what the media has trained him to believe is the way to buy a home.

Don't try to counter every term as well as price. Keep it simple. Focus on the most important things. Price may be your most important objective so be willing to compromise on other details if you can get a price you find acceptable.

On the other hand, if the price is low but the closing will take place quickly, with minimal contingencies, you might be well-advised to accept the low price in order to be able to move on with your life.

Inspection contingencies

The first contingency most sellers face is the home inspection. A professional, licensed inspector will make an appointment to inspect your home. Other specialized inspectors may also make appointments.

During that inspection period your home will have its plumbing, electrical system, heating and air conditioning, roof, and structure evaluated. The home might also be evaluated for the presence of lead-based paint, asbestos, radon, termites, or mold. In some areas there may be other types of inspections as well.

Normally, the standard is that all systems should be operating in the manner in which they were originally intended to operate. So if the air conditioning is working but not cooling properly, that is not working as it was intended to operate. If a window is painted shut, that is not how it was intended to work.

Following these inspections you should receive a copy of the reports, a detailed list of any deficiencies, along with a request from the buyer that repairs be made on those items. Depending on how the contract was written, you may be expected to repair any or all of those things.

The terms of the contract may allow you to refuse to make repairs and thus release the buyer from the obligation to go through with the contract. In that case the home goes back on the market and you begin your search for a buyer all over again. The contract may also state that if you make all repairs then the buyer has no alternative but to go forward with the contract.

You may have filled out a Sellers Disclosure, when you listed the home, which stated what you knew to be wrong with the home at that time. The inspection report now gives you knowledge of things of which you may have been unaware. With that knowledge, you would be required to disclose all of those facts to any potential new buyer if this contract falls through. That new buyer, armed with that knowledge, may decide not to even make an offer on the home.

So you can deal with those issues now or later, but you will end up dealing with them. It's better to continue working through an existing contract if at all possible than it is to start all over again and wait for another prospective buyer to write a contract. If you are able to make this one work out you can get on with the sale.

Mortgage contingencies

Most buyers purchase a home using a mortgage, as opposed to paying cash. If that's the case on your contract, the buyer will need to have the mortgage approved before they can go through with the sale.

This approval represents a contingency in the contract. This means that if, for whatever reason, the buyer does not get the approval for the mortgage, the contract is void and any monies held in escrow would generally be returned to the buyer. The approval may hinge on the buyer's income verification, credit report, employment, or other factors.

Ideally, your buyer will have already applied for a mortgage and been approved, subject to the appraisal on your home. However, that's usually not the case. In many cases, your buyer has not even made application for the mortgage.

Usually, one of the terms on the contract is the time frame for the buyer to make application. If the time frame on the contract is longer than a week for that to take place you can counter a shorter period of time.

Unless the buyer has unusual circumstances the period of loan approval in most areas should be 30 days or less. If the buyer's contract has a longer period than that you can counter a shorter time frame or ask why it needs to be so long.

Closing Date contingencies

Most sellers want a quick closing. So you have the right to ask for a closing soon after the mortgage approval. Be sure to allow at least a week between the mortgage approval and closing. If they are back to back you may have to book a mover and get out before you even know if the loan is approved.

From Contract to Closing

You've agreed to a price and terms with your buyer. Now any contingencies in the contract have to be met. Very few of them are within your control. There may be copies of prior title insurance or a previous survey you are expected to deliver. However, most of the contingencies are in the buyer's hands.

If you have an agent, your agent should be tracking the deadlines for each contingency and will keep you up to date. If you are selling the home yourself you should make a check list with dates that each task is to be completed.

You will need to make the home available for inspections so plan on being flexible for those. The inspectors have their own schedules and you need to be able to accommodate their time frames. If there are multiple inspections to be done there may have to be multiple times set. It's unlikely that they will all be available to do their inspections at the same time.

If there is a second binder deposit due, you or your agent needs to ensure that it is delivered on time and deposited in the appropriate escrow account.

When due dates for any of the contingencies are not met, it is up to you or your agent to follow through. This is where many agents earn their commission, by staying on top of dates and keeping the transaction on track. Many contracts fall through or have unintended consequences for the buyer or seller who misses a due date.

Closing and Moving

Everything has gone according to plan. The contract was accepted, the mortgage approved, inspections were done, repairs made, and contingencies were met. The mover has been scheduled and you have begun to pack up.

It is expected that you will turn over the home in the condition it was on the day the contract was written, so be sure that you do just that. You must maintain the yard, the plants, the home itself, right up until closing.

Don't try to save money by not watering the lawn or shutting off the utilities. If a mold problem occurs because you tried to skimp on air conditioning, you'll be expected to repair that before closing can occur.

The buyer is entitled to do a "walk through" right before closing and the home should be in the expected condition. Most contracts stipulate that the seller will leave everything about the home clean, with no trash or possessions remaining. If you have items you think the buyer might want, be sure you have discussed that prior to closing and leave ONLY those items.

The actual closing of escrow may take place in an attorney's office or at a title company or in the real estate agent's office. The location doesn't matter. In some states it is common for both buyer and seller to be present. In other areas the closings are handled separately. You will be advised of all the details well in advance.

You should have also received a copy of the HUD-1 statement in the days immediately prior to closing. That is the official detailed statement of all costs for each side of the transaction and how the net proceeds for the seller were calculated. Be sure to review the HUD-1 in detail and have all your questions answered before you attend the closing.

Now It's Over

You and the buyer have signed all the appropriate documents and it's done. Keys are turned over. The For Sale sign has come down. Time to move on with your life.

Many people reach this point and feel they should beat themselves up. Did I sell for too little? Did I hold on too long? There may be a million other questions that will run through your head.

In the long run, you did everything right. You've sold your home in a down market when many other homeowners could not sell theirs. Be grateful that you can move on with your life. You can enjoy the memories of your past home as you move on to make new memories in a next phase of your life.

www.ingramcontent.com/pod-product-compliance
Lightning Source LLC
Chambersburg PA
CBHW071236170526
45165CB00003B/1115

* 9 7 8 1 4 4 0 1 0 4 5 9 6 *